# Spire Study System

capture. cross-train. conquer.

# IELTS

## ACADEMIC
## PRACTICE TESTS

IELTS General Training Book with
Reading, Writing, & Listening Test Prep
Questions for the IELTS Exam

# Contents

# Preparing for the IELTS

The first step to prepare for the IELTS is to know what to expect on the exam. We will review each of the 3 parts of the test and explain what you need to know and how you will need to answer the questions. We will also provide some tips and ideas to help you study and prepare.

## What to know about Part 1: The Listening Section

This part of the test will last 30 minutes and has 40 questions total. You will listen to 4 separate recordings of native English speakers that you will be asked 10 questions about immediately after each recording. The 10 questions are designed so that the answer choices appear in the order you heard from start to end of the recording.

These are the recordings you will hear:
- **Recording 1** – a conversation between two people set in an everyday social context.
- **Recording 2** - a speech by one person, called a "monologue", set in a normal everyday social context, e.g. a speech about local facilities.
- **Recording 3** – a conversation between up to four people set in an educational or training context, e.g. a university tutor and a student discussing an assignment.
- **Recording 4** - a speech by one person on an academic subject, like a teacher or professor giving a lecture.

There are a few different types and formats of question you will have to answer, such as multiple choice, fill in the blank, sentence completion, completing a chart, or short answer summary. None of the answer types require any special skill or knowledge to correctly complete them, but take time *to read the instructions very carefully!* Sometimes you will be given a limit of words, such as "write no more than one word to complete the sentence". If you write more than one word in that example, you will lose points. Other instructions might tell you "no more than 3 words or numbers", in which case you do not *need* to write 3 words, only that you *cannot write more*. You will *not* lose points for writing fewer than 3 words or numbers, but you *will lose points* if you write 4 or more. It is of course important in all questions that your writing is neat, easy to read, and spelled correctly.

As for the type of information you will be asked about in the questions, there are 4 main concepts of your listening skills being tested. Here are some examples and explanations of what you can expect:

**Specific Facts:** An example would be "What did the speaker say about the red car?". This is a very basic question and one of the easier types. You do not need to understand the emotion or interpret opinions, only recall exactly what the speaker said. In this example, the speaker might have said "I sold my red car yesterday". Your answer choices might include incorrect options such as "I wrecked my red car", "my mom has a red car", etc.

**Main idea**: This is the next level of difficulty, where you must interpret the purpose of the speaker's message. This requires you to take the entire recording in mind and summarize it into one sentence. You want to use "context clues" which is words that give you a hint on the subject being talked about. For example, if someone is talking about eating only a vegetarian diet, they could making a statement that it is "good" and "healthy" and other positive words. Or perhaps they use words like "unhealthy" and say things like "not enough protein" and other negative words. It is important to read the answer choices *very carefully*, because the choices in this example could include "A vegetarian diet is healthier than other diets" vs. "A vegetarian diet is <u>not</u> healthier than other diets".

**Opinions and Attitudes**: This is the next most difficult type of question. You won't be asked to recall a specific fact or statement, but you have to interpret something new. Let's use the example from above regarding vegetarian diets. The question you might be asked is "If offered a choice, which of the 4 choices would the speaker most likely choose for lunch?" followed by "A) Pork Sandwich  B) Salad C) Fish D) Beef Stew". While none of those items were mentioned in the recording, you will have to interpret that someone who is a vegetarian would only eat one of those items.

**Specific Words**: This is the most difficult type of question. You will be asked what the meaning of a specific word from the recording, based on the context in which it was used. As you know, many words in the English language can have multiple meanings depending on how and when they are used. Here are some examples: the word "right" could be a direction, such as "Turn right at the next street" but it also can be used to mean "correct" such as "she chose the right answer". Another example is "type". You can use "type" to specify one thing from another such as "that's not the type of shirt I like" or of course it also relates to a computer such as "I need to type a letter to send."

# What to know about Part 2: The Reading Section

The Reading section takes 60 minutes and consists of 40 questions.

While you have the advantage of referring back to the text to help you find answers, the questions in the Reading section will be more difficult and require you to interpret information from context. You will be tested on your ability of:

- Reading for gist or main idea
- Reading for detail
- Skimming or summarizing
- Understanding arguments
- Identifying opinions and attitudes
- Identifying the writer's purpose

There will be 3 sections within this part of the test. The text passages you will read are designed to resemble text from books, magazines, newspapers, notices, advertisements, company handbooks and guidelines. All of these are styles of writing and types of information are things you would have to read in everyday life.

**The first section** is referred to as "social survival". These are text passages where you need to obtain basic facts and information you would use in normal social life. For example, identifying the correct date, time, or location from newspaper advertisements.

**The second section** is referred to as "Workplace survival". This section focuses on types of text you would need to understand to read a job description, understand instructions for applying for a job, and reading company manuals or handbooks once you have started your employment.

**The third section** is referred to as "General Reading". This section is most difficult and contains all types of reading passages. These passages could come from any book or narrative, magazine article, and be fiction or non-fiction. The questions here are more about descriptive information than facts. Like in the "Listening" section, there are different styles of questions. Along with multiple choice, you will be asked to write short answers, fill in blanks, complete charts or label diagrams. Again, none of these require any special knowledge or skills to understand how to complete them. The instructions will always be clear but is *it critically important that you read the instructions carefully for each question*! Again, the question might say "using no more than 3 words or numbers" and you will lose points if you use more than what is asked. You will also lose points for spelling incorrectly and if your writing cannot be read.

# What to know about Part 3: The Writing Section

The writing section lasts 60 minutes and includes 2 "tasks". In each task, you will be given some form of information, then prompted to write a few paragraphs with specific instructions. Each task however has different context and requires a different type of writing.

## Task 1

You will be given information and asked to explain it. This could be a graph or a chart, or any piece of information. You might also be given a prompt and instructed to write a letter to someone. In either case, your essay or letter is testing your ability to explain facts of a specific topic, or request information on a specific topic. The letter could be formal like you would write to your employer or can be informal such as you would write to a friend or family member.

Your writing must be neat and legible, and you will lose points for incorrect spelling. You must write at least 150 words! Remember, while you do not lose points for going over 150 words, it will take away time you have for task 2. When you practice, be sure to become familiar with how long it takes you to write 150 words, so that you can intentionally plan what you want to write that is long enough.

## Task 2

Unlike task 1, you are not writing a letter to anyone. You are instead given a statement or asked a question and instructed to write an essay arguing a point of view. You can write in a more personal style.

The topics here are all very general, but always something that you can choose one side or the other. Which side you choose is not important and does not affect your score at all. Some simple examples of prompts might about things like "Is getting a college degree more important now than 20 years ago?" or "Should people get a tax benefit for driving more fuel-efficient cars?". Again, while there is no "right" or "wrong" side to choose, your writing must be on topic and relevant to the question asked.

This section requires a minimum of 250 words. You will lose points for being under 250 words but are allowed to write more. You will of course lose points for incorrect spelling as well, and your writing must be neat and legible. This section will take about twice as long as Task 1 because it is not only a longer response but requires more thought to plan out a well formed thought.

You want your ideas to be organized. If you randomly go from topic to topic, or do not complete your thoughts or arguments, you will be penalized. When you make an argument, it is important to give an example to support it. Here is an example, if you decided to respond to the example prompt above that "I do not think college is more important than 20 years ago", you could include an example that a family member of yours did not attend college but instead went to a trade school and after a few years of training and mastering a skill, now manages a very successful business. Other friends or family members however did go to college and now have trouble finding a job because they lack a specific skill. Please note that that is a very brief summary of what you might want to write, and you would of course want to give much more detail and elaborate to reinforce your argument. Also, it is important to note that these examples do not have to be from your life! You can make up arguments or examples, as long as it is realistic and not silly.

**Scoring Factors for the Writing Section**

Task 1 responses are assessed on:
Task achievement
- Is the response relevant to the prompt? Does it accurately respond to the question asked or follow the instructions given? Were at last 150 words used?

Coherence and cohesion
- Is the writing organized logically by idea or context? Are thoughts completed and ideas linked together?

Lexical resource
- What is the range of vocabulary used in the writing?

Grammatical range and accuracy.
- Is there correct spelling and usage of words?

Task 2 responses are assessed on:
Task response
- Is the essay response relevant to what was asked? Did the writer take a position or choose a side? Did the writer give good examples that supported their statements or opinion?

Coherence and cohesion
- Is the writing organized logically by idea or context? Are thoughts completed and ideas linked together?

Lexical resource
- What is the range of vocabulary used in the writing?

Grammatical range and accuracy.
- Is there correct spelling and usage of words?

**Strategy for Writing Section**

Take 5 Minutes First
With time ticking away, it is hard not to jump in and immediately start writing but stopping to think first is a crucial step. Taking 5 minutes to plan your essay out will save you the trouble of realizing you were struggling to make your point and your essay is not organized, and now it is too late to go back and revise.

Spend the first 5 minutes thinking about the issue, the perspectives, and your own views. What can you use as evidence? Is this issue like any other issue in terms of how it might be handled or mishandled? Is there anything in your own life that you can use as evidence? When it comes to the other perspectives, where do the arguments break down? Are there any logic problems? Do the perspectives work in some cases but not all? Answers to these questions give you an angle to start your writing, but it takes a few moments to think up some answers. So take them.

## Make a Plan

If you like to write outlines, great. Write your thesis and jot down your ideas. If you don't, no problem; however, you still need to have your position and support set in your head. So write it down or don't, but make sure you have a good handle on what you're arguing and where you're headed with the essay.

## Have a Few Templates in Mind

If writing leaves you frozen like a deer in the headlights, you might find it easier to have a few templates already in mind – roadmaps, if you will, that provide the overall structure. Your job is to fill in the places on the map where you're going to stop and ponder. Keep in mind, this is a basic framework. The more savvy you are with writing, the more you will move beyond this template. But for those of you who don't like the idea of timed writing, you will benefit from knowing you have a solid place to start the writing process.

Here's an example template:

- **Paragraph 1**: Use an opening sentence to get the reader's attention. State your position or opinion. In two or three more sentences briefly discuss your main points.
- **Paragraph 2**: Use this paragraph to support your opinion. Have a topic sentence, an example, and a summary of the point.
- **Paragraph 3**: Use this paragraph to either bring up another point to support your position, or to compare your position to the opposite argument with examples that further help your argument. Use the same format as the previous paragraph – topic sentence, example, summary.
- **Paragraph 4**: Use this paragraph as your conclusion. Restate your topic opinion, summarize your arguments, and present a strong ending.

## Pay Attention to the Particulars, but Don't Let Them Overwhelm You

Try to leave a minute or two to reread your essay at the end. Use the sub-vocalization technique. This means that you read as if you are pretending reading out loud, or as if you are reading to another person. It has been proven that you will catch more errors by reading this way than simply reading with your eyes alone. Check for grammar problems, missing words, sentence fragments, and spelling errors.

Remember, you do not need to use big words to earn a high score. Sometimes trying to use words you do not normally use can work against you – you might spell them incorrectly or use them in the wrong context. No matter what, they will stick out and draw attention because they don't fit with the rest of the essay. Write cleanly, clearly, and coherently.

**Take a Breath**

Really, take a breath. This essay is more about quantity than quality. By quantity I don't mean the number of words, but rather the content. Do you provide an argument? Do you mention the three different perspectives? Do you offer concrete proof for your viewpoint (concrete means a solid example as opposed to a vague statement that something is true because you said so)? Do you have an introduction with a thesis, body paragraphs with evidence and explanation, and a conclusion?

Sounds a lot like the template above. Practice coming up with a few different templates to have at the ready, and you are already halfway there.

# TASK 1 SAMPLE PROMPT and SAMPLE RESPONSE

Prompt: What makes people happy? There are two charts below of different age groups. Write 150 words or more summarizing the information and making comparisons or identifying differences.

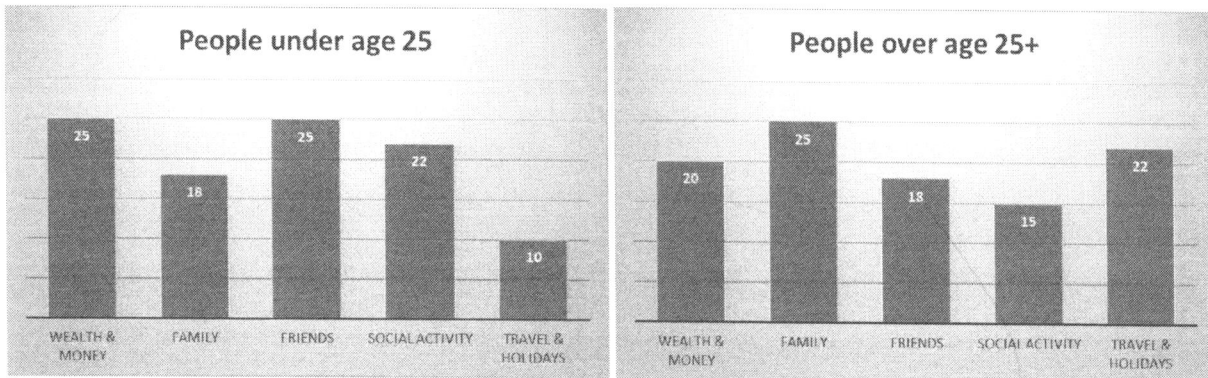

While there are certainly some similarities between the two groups, there are some important differences worth noting.

First, we will review the similarities. In both groups, we see that Wealth & Money are important factors. 25% of the younger group and 20% of the older group indicate that it is what brings them most happiness. The next similarities are found in the groupings of Family and Friends. While 25% of people under the age of 25 responded that Friends are most important for happiness, those over age 25 had a 25% response that Family is most important.

Let us now review the differences between the two groups. The largest difference in responses is found in Travel & Holidays. Only 10% of the younger group chose this option. However, the older group responded at 22%. The other significant disparity in responses is in Social Activity. The younger group responded at 22%, while the older group only had 15%. In fact, the largest deviation between responses of the groups is Social Activity and Travel & Holidays.

(174 words)

# TASK 2 SAMPLE PROMPT AND EXAMPLE RESPONSES

What motivates us to work? There are two perspectives to consider:

- More than basic needs: A person out of a job will be motivated by the need for basic survival of food and a home. One who is gainfully employed but does not feel professionally fulfilled will be motivated by a need for esteem.
- Fear or reward: Some workers are motivated by a desire to achieve more money, more power, or more praise. Others act and react only out of fear of being fired or getting in trouble.

Which of these perspectives do you agree with?  Gives reasons and examples.

I think people are motivated if their getting what they want. Like what the one guy says that if their satisfyed they'll work hard to get what they want and if your not happy you dont want to do nothing. My uncle bob hasnt worked for a long time cause he says his bosses dont ever appricate what he does anyhow so why bother. my teachers dont like how i act sometimes and they get really mean if i dont do my homework and if theyd chill out a little id probly work harder and like rite now im hungry when im hungry its hard to focus on my lesson when i didn't have brekfast or i staid up to late the nite before. So my perseptive is     i think everybodys gotta get food and sleep to feel good enough to work and also like uncle bob need to be appricated.

## Scoring Explanation for a score of 1

*Task response = 1*

> The essay is fewer than 250 words, and there is no cohesive thesis that the essay works to support. Although the writer presents the idea that people are motivated to get what they want, the essay does not go on to fully support that idea.

*Coherence and cohesion = 1*

> Although there is some development, the example of Uncle Bob and the writer's response to his teachers, the essay is still a random collection of unrelated ideas.

*Lexical resource = 1*

> There is no paragraphing or grouping of ideas and small range of vocabulary.

*Grammatical range and accuracy = 1*

> There are numerous errors in usage, mechanics, and punctuation. Much of the word choice is simplistic and colloquial, which weakens the argument tremendously.

What motivates people to work hard? I think people work hard because of something they want. If someone wants something then they'll go for it.

Sometimes people work hard because their in need. If I need to fix my car well then I'll ask for more hours at my job. But they also might work hard just because that's what we're supposed to do. I work hard sometimes because my parents say I should. So if people have a need then they'll step up and do whatever they can to fill that need.

People also work hard to get a goal which is sort of like working for a need but maybe different. This is more like if they want a raise or a promotion of something like that. And in reverse they might work hard because their afraid they'll lose their job. So working because of fear or incentives may also be true.

Finally, I agree people work for satisfaction and dissatisfaction. I try to work hard on my school work because my parents want me to and I like to get as good of grades as I can. Bad grades mean I'm dissatisfied and I've let my parents down.

In conclusion, I agree with all the perspectives and think their all right in different ways. Basicly, I think its true that people work to get what they want.

## Scoring Explanation for a score of 3

*Task Response = 3*

This essay is only 230 words and has a narrow scope with limited ideas presented. Instead, he simply states the given perspectives and attempts to give examples. Rather than building an argument, the analysis is loosely connected with the given perspectives, reflecting a weakness in both thought and purpose.

*Coherence and cohesion = 3*

Weak development fails to support and clarify this argument. In fact, the rest of the argument meanders off in different directions as the writer attempts to address each of the given perspectives. There is no real explanation of ideas, nor does the writer consider the implications of the perspectives within each paragraph.

*Lexical resource = 3*

Although the writer provides paragraphing in an attempt to structure his essay, the ideas are grouped with no clear connection. There is a minimum amount of vocabulary range.

*Grammatical range and accuracy = 3*

Awkward word choices throughout the essay make it difficult to understand. (If I need to fix my car well then I'll ask for more hours. People...work hard to get a goal which I guess is sort of like working for a need but maybe different. Bad grades mean I'm dissatisfied...) There are a few other errors in spelling, punctuation and sentence structure that show a weakness in language use and weaken the overall argument.

People are motivated in different ways. Motivation is important and there are lots of different reasons why people want to do well. People are motivated in good ways and bad ways and that effects how they perform in their jobs and in school.

Some people are motivated because of their needs they don't have but they want. If someone has food and water, safety, and love, then having self-esteem can be something they work toward. If someone doesn't have self-esteem, then that becomes important to them. They will be motivated to do well in their job and earn praise and maybe even a raise so they can feel good about themselves.

In either work or in life, people can also be motivated by either incentives or fear. Some people want to achieve more money or more power or more respect. Others might work hard at their jobs or in school because they are afraid of being fired or getting in trouble in their classes. Either way, they work harder so that they can achieve more and so they won't have any negative consequences.

Lastly, people are motivated based on whether they are satisfied or dissatisfied. If they have achievement, recognition and advancement in their jobs, they are satisfied and will continue to work hard to keep these things because it makes them feel good and satisfied. If they don't like their jobs or aren't making a good salary or maybe don't like the people they work with then they are dissatisfied and won't work as hard. If their bosses know how they feel then they can maybe do things that will make them feel better, which will make them more satisfied and they will work harder.

In conclusion, people are motivated in different ways. They are motivated in good and bad ways and that effects how they do. It's important to understand how people are motivated so their bosses in charge of them can inspire them to achieve.

## Scoring Explanation for a score of 6

*Task Response = 6*

> The writer clearly states an opinion and made valid, logical arguments. It gives the reader some sense of direction, but the essay is more simplistic than it could have been. The writer could have compared and contrasted the other perspectives more, rather the essay relies on repeating and agreeing with their claims. Although the writer tries to include examples- the idea that some people work not to be fired or not to get into trouble in classes - the analysis does not lend itself to supporting the writer's thesis.

*Coherence and cohesion = 6*

> The essay is structured correctly, but the writer misses opportunities to make meaningful connections from one topic paragraph to the next.

*Lexical resource = 6*

> The essay is somewhat repetitive and the example requires the reader to make his own inferences of how and why fear (of losing one's job or getting in trouble in school) can be motivational. A broader selection of word choice could have helped elaborate these points.

*Grammatical range and accuracy = 6*

> There are a few misused word forms and grammar errors (that effects how they perform, if someone doesn't have…it becomes important to them). The ideas are clearly communicated, but the basic language does nothing to clarify or strengthen the argument. Occasional awkwardness in sentence structure (so their bosses in charge of them, their needs they don't have but want) show a limited level of skill in language use.

As more and more of society seems to be unmotivated, schools and employers have had to find ways to push people to do a good job. There are multiple theories of how to do that, and although motivating people is essential for schools and businesses to do, there is a question of how they can accomplish that goal. I believe that the best way to motivate others is by making them feel good about themselves, which can be done with incentives and with satisfaction.

The world has become a more complicated, perplexing place. People have to work harder than ever before to do well and to make a living, and that is because there is so much competition. In schools, students must work exceptionally hard to maintain a high grade point average and a high class rank. They are competing with all their classmates to have high scores. In their jobs, people have to toil endlessly and often endure long hours to make sure they are doing the very best job they can. Otherwise, there may be someone else standing in line to take their job away from them. If a worker cannot produce an acceptable amount of products on an assembly line, for example, he will lose his job to his competition. Therefore, he must be motivated.

Only when people feel good about themselves do they have the self-esteem needed to try to achieve. If someone doesn't like himself and doesn't feel worthy, he is less likely to feel like pushing himself toward a goal. However, individuals who have a high self- esteem feel as though they are worthy. That same worker will have confidence that he can not only meet but exceed the number of products he's expected to produce, and then he'll be able to do so.

Incentives can be motivational, but fear is only a hindrance to motivation. Motivating with incentives is really just like motivating with self-esteem. When a person is rewarded for good performance, in school or at his job, he gains self-respect and confidence so he'll work even harder. He will want to feel even better about himself and want to keep receiving the incentives. In school, a student who gets an A feels good and wants to get more A's. Similarly, at work, a person who gets a raise feels good and wants to get another raise. Therefore, incentives lead to people to a higher self-esteem, which, in turn, creates both job satisfaction and future motivation.

*Task Response = 9*

> The writer has a clear argument that engages the options presented in the prompt, then explores his thesis with examples and explanation (in school and in the workplace.) The writer also addresses the complexity of the issue. (Only when people feel good about themselves do they have the self-esteem needed to try to achieve. Incentives can be motivational but fear is only a hindrance to motivation.)

*Coherence and cohesion = 9*

> The essay revolves around a clear organizational structure. The introduction identifies the opinion of the writer, and the writer uses the second paragraph to begin to build an argument that motivation is important, setting the essay up to explore how best to achieve motivation in the following paragraphs. Paragraphs three and four drive the argument forward with specific examples and discussion of the complicating evidence that fear is a hindrance to motivation.

*Lexical Resource = 9*

> Transitions are used well to connect ideas, most prevalently within the paragraphs (otherwise, therefore, similarly, however).

*Grammatical range and accuracy = 9*

> The writer has a firm grip on writing conventions and uses the language in a way that contributes to both the clarity and the overall effect of the essay. Strong word choices, such as perplexing, toil and endure emphasize the writer's arguments without becoming redundant. There is a varied sentence style, which increases the readers' interest and creates a logic that helps to clarify and support the thesis.

# Listening Practice Test

Please visit the following website on your computer, tablet or smartphone to complete the listening sections of this book.

# www.listen-ielts.com

**We want this to be as easy as possible for our students to prepare for the IELTS. That is why we decided that:**

- **This resource is entirely free for your use.**
- **You do not have to sign up or create a login.**
- **You do not have to provide any personal information.**
- **You may download the audio to your device so you can use it later without Internet connection.**

# IELTS Listening practice questions

**Recording #1**: The first recording is a conversation between a female student and a male student. Listen to the recording ONCE, and then immediately answer questions 1-10.

1.  *Fill in the blank to complete this sentence:*

    The female speakers mother went to a _____ last week.

2.  Where was the speaker's mother last week?
    a.  Arizona
    b.  Albuquerque
    c.  Alabama
    d.  Utah

3.  The speaker's mother complained of pain in her:
    a.  Knees
    b.  Back
    c.  Hands
    d.  Shoulders

4.  The female speaker stated that her mother is usually very healthy.
    a.  True
    b.  False

5.  Her mother had to climb up and down a lot of:
    a.  Ramps
    b.  Stairs
    c.  Escalators
    d.  Uneven sidewalks

6. What was the mother's difficulty with attending the presentations?
    a. She could not find the correct room.
    b. She had difficulty hearing the speakers.
    c. She was late because her watch broke.
    d. Going up and down stairs hurt her knees.

7. *Fill in the blank to complete this sentence:*

    The male speaker says he is from _____.

8. The male speaker says the altitude is over _____ feet high where he is from.
    a. 1,000
    b. 2,000
    c. 3,000
    d. 7,000

9. When tourists get altitude sickness, all of the following happen EXCEPT
    a. It usually lasts several days.
    b. It causes breathing problems.
    c. They feel a little sick.
    d. They pass out and lose consciousness.

10. According to the male speaker, altitude sickness usually passes in a few _____.
    a. Weeks
    b. Hours
    c. Minutes
    d. Days

**Recording #2:**

The second recording is of one male speaker doing a monologue about traveling. Listen to the recording ONCE, and then immediately answer questions 11-20.

11. At the beginning of recording, where did the speaker say he has backpacked before?
    a. Europe
    b. Uruguay
    c. Uganda
    d. East Asia

12. The speaker indicated he enjoys traveling alone because of which of the following:
    a. It encourages him to communicate with the local people
    b. It is less expensive
    c. He does not enjoy being with other travelers
    d. He is traveling for work and must focus

13. In 3 or fewer words, describe where would the speaker write his observations in his notebook?

    _____

14. True or False: the speaker would often forget to write in his notebook as he spent more time talking to the other diners?
    a. True
    b. False

15. In 3 or fewer words, describe one drawback of traveling alone that the speaker mentioned.

    _____

16. Based on your interpretation of everything the speaker said, which of the following is an opinion he is most likely to share:
    a. It is dangerous to travel alone, so only experienced travelers should try it.
    b. Traveling with a group is more fun, but if no one else wants to go, traveling alone is OK.
    c. You should try traveling alone because you have a different opportunity to meet new people.
    d. Traveling alone is only fun if you backpack by yourself.

17. The speaker said that in the future, he intends to backpack travel to:
    a. Egypt
    b. Canada
    c. South America
    d. None of the above

18. Based on your interpretation of the opinions expressed by the speaker, which of the following is the holiday or vacation he would most likely choose?
    a. A cruise ship from his own country
    b. A luxury hotel resort vacation with family
    c. A trip to a foreign country he has visited before
    d. A trip to a new foreign country alone

19. True or False: The speaker thinks it is great to travel alone, except that he would prefer to have a group so he did not have to make decisions alone.
    a. True
    b. False

20. *Fill in the blank to complete the sentence below:*

The speaker said that it is more _____ to stay in a hotel room by yourself.

**Recording #3:**

The second recording of a male and female speaker having a discussion. Listen to the recording ONCE, and then immediately answer questions 21-30.

21. What are the speakers mainly discussing?
    a. How the woman should prepare for her class.
    b. The woman's responsibilities at home.
    c. The plans to widen the highway near the school.
    d. Different events of everyday life.

22. Who is difficult for the female speaker to please?
    a. The male speaker
    b. Her boss
    c. Her parents
    d. Her mom

*#23 & #24: use the below question to answer both questions #23 and #24.*

   **Why does the male speaker believe that the widening of the highway will cause difficulties for him to get to school?**

23. Choose one correct answer below:
    a. The roads will be narrower.
    b. There will be more traffic.
    c. There will be many bicycles on the roads.
    d. There will be fewer exits.

24. Choose the 2nd correct answer below:
    a. The roads will be narrower.
    b. There will be more traffic.
    c. There will be many bicycles on the roads.
    d. There will be fewer exits.

25. What does the male student mean when he says: *"on the dot at 10"*?
    a. The test begins around 10.
    b. The test begins precisely at 10.
    c. The test will start as soon as the students arrive for their 10 class.
    d. The test at approximately 10 o'clock.

26. Why does the man mean when he says: 'we will have to get up earlier and leave home earlier'?
    a. It will take him longer to travel to school because of traffic police.
    b. The roads will be more congested because of more exits.
    c. He expects the next year's classes to begin earlier.
    d. The man thinks construction will cause traffic delays.

27. According to the recording, what is flan?
    a. A cooked banana.
    b. An appetizer.
    c. A dessert.
    d. Heaven in your mouth

28. What does the man's favorite sport?
    a. Soccer
    b. Football
    c. Cycling
    d. Basketball

29. Why does the woman find it difficult to do her job at the restaurant well?
    a. Because her boss is very demanding.
    b. Because she has a poor memory.
    c. Because the boss is always complaining.
    d. Because they get very busy at times.

30. *Fill in the blank to complete the following sentence:*

The female speaker said that her family's favorite food is beans and rice, and they come from the country of _____.

The fourth recording is part of a lecture from a science class. Listen to the recording ONCE, and then immediately answer questions 31-40.

31. What is the lecture mainly about?
    a. Innovations in nanotechnology
    b. A comparison of nanotechnology and previous technology.
    c. The ethics of nanotechnology
    d. Problems with nanotechnology.

32. In what way is nanotechnology different from previous technology?
    a. It is smaller.
    b. It is microscopic.
    c. It is larger.
    d. It is huge.

33. According to the professor, which one of the following options is an actual nanotechnology product in use today?
    a. Clothing that can wash itself.
    b. Bandages that kill bacteria by eliminating their food source.
    c. Scratch-proof paint for cars.
    d. Glass that can clean itself.

34. In his next class, the professor will lecture about all of the following EXCEPT
    a. Creating a new race of humans
    b. The economics of nanotechnology
    c. The ethics of more lethal weapons
    d. The need for smaller medical devices

35. *Fill in the blank to complete the following sentence.*

    A probe is being used in cardiology centers around the world to get images from inside a patient's _____.

36. According to the professor, the layer of Zinc-Oxide protects against what?
    a. Coffee stains
    b. Blood stains
    c. UV radiation
    d. Bleach

37. True or False: While a tennis racket with nano-tube infused graphite is very light, but is not as strong as traditional steel or aluminum rackets.
    a. True
    b. False

38. *Fill in the blank to complete the following sentence:*

    Some scientists believe that nanoparticles could be dangerous to humans because they could pass from the bloodstream to the _____.

39. True or False: An advantage that helps scientists is that on a nano-scale, atoms in larger groups act very similarly as they do in small groups.
    a. True
    b. False

40. The tennis ball created by Wilson has a double core, one of which is made of _____ nanoparticles:
    a. Rubber
    b. Titanium
    c. Clay
    d. Graphite

# Reading Practice Tests

**Part 3**

**Reading Comprehension**

Directions: Read the passage. Then answer the questions.

| | |
|---|---|
| 1 | No one knows exactly how chocolate was discovered. Approximately, one thousand years ago, somewhere in Central America, the Mayan Indians began to roast the odd shaped fruit and use the seeds in a drink called *chocolatl* or *xocoatl*. This "bitter water" has evolved into what we know today as hot chocolate. |
| 2 | Historians believe that the way to use and enjoy the cocoa fruit was discovered over 2500 years ago. The fruit was probably used for the pulp which was slightly acidic. Later the beans or seeds were roasted and **pulverized** to make a thick, **coarse** paste. This paste was flavored with different seeds, vanilla, chilies and honey. After the paste was flavored, it was allowed to dry. The chocolate paste became hard and could easily be transported by the natives in rectangular shapes called tablets. The natives used the chocolate tablets to make a drink by dissolving the tablets in water and whipping it until frothy. |
| 3 | Columbus discovered chocolate on his fourth trip to the Americas. He did not like the drink as prepared by the natives. Yet, he realized the beans were valuable to the Mayans because they rushed to pick up some beans that fell when the Spaniards were loading their ship with **them**. He carried some beans back to King Ferdinand V of Spain who was not impressed with them at first. |
| 4 | Hernan Cortez discovered also the value of the cocoa beans when he found Moctezuma's treasury. He had expected to find gold, but instead he found more than one billion cocoa beans. The Spaniard realized they were valuable, but he wasn't sure exactly how. |
| 5 | Cortez learned how to prepare chocolate and carried his knowledge back to Spain where it remained unpopular. In 1530 and 1540, the nuns at the Guanaco convent in South America began adding sugar and vanilla to the drink. This made the drink more popular to the European palate. |
| 6 | For almost 100 years, Spain and her colonies maintained a **monopoly** on the cocoa beans. In 1606, the monopoly ended and other European nations began to obtain the cocoa beans and produce chocolate. |
| 7 | The cocoa beverage became very popular in Europe through the royal courts and the nobility. Chocolate houses were the rage, yet the drink would probably not appeal to us today. The drink was thick, acrid, and greasy. |
| 8 | Many attempts were made to eliminate the bitterness and oiliness by adding wheat, corn or oat flour. Nothing worked until Coenraad van Houten invented a hydraulic press that could extract two thirds of the fat. The press had two great advantages. It could eliminate most of the fat which could be used to make chocolate for eating, and it could use the remains of the paste for grinding into cocoa powder. The alkalizing process, called *dutching*, allowed the powder to remain suspended in liquids for longer periods of time. |
| 9 | The manufacture of modern chocolate candy began over 150 years ago in Sweden by the Swiss brothers Cloetta who built their Steam-Chocolate-Factory in the city of Malmo. When another Swiss discovered how to manufacture milk solids, the milk chocolate candy bar was |

| | created. |
|---|---|
| 10 | In modern times, chocolate **confections** became a billion dollar industry. The world's biggest consumer of chocolate is Switzerland with an average of 19.8 pounds per person followed by Germany at 17.4 pounds. The United States comes in ninth on this chart with only 9.5 pounds per person. According to Statista in 2016, worldwide chocolate confectionery consumption was a staggering 7.3 million tons in 2015-2016. Milk chocolate is the preferred flavor with over 50% of the market. |
| 11 | Even though cocoa beans were discovered in the Americas, more than two-thirds of the world's production comes from West Africa. The largest company in the world that manufactures and sells chocolate and cocoa products is Barry Callebaut. This wholesaler, a business-to-business (b2b) entity, produces chocolate that appears in one of five products around the world. About 42% and 26% of their chocolate products are sold to Europe and America respectively of an astonishing 1.8 million tonnes. |
| | |
| | |
| Sources | Young, A.M. The chocolate tree—a natural history of chocolate. Washington: Smithsonian Institute Press.<br>Barry Callebaut website: https://www.barry-callebaut.com/at-a-glance |

Directions: Answer the following questions.

1. The word "pulverized" in paragraph 2 is closest in meaning to

    A. carefully preserved
    B. decimated
    C. destroyed
    D. crushed

2. The word "coarse" in paragraph 2 is closest in meaning to

    A. rough
    B. consisting of large particles
    C. fine or delicate
    D. uneven

3. Which of the following made the tablets easy to transport?

    A. The tablets were hard and dry.
    B. The tablets were stackable.
    C. The tablets were small.
    D. The tablets were easily broken.

4. What can be inferred from paragraph 1 and 2 as reasons King Ferdinand V did not like the chocolate drink?

    A.  The drink was not well prepared
    B.  His friends did not like the drink either.
    C.  The drink was bitter.
    D.  The flavors were unusual.

5.  What does the word them in paragraph 3 refer to?

    A.  Beans
    B.  Natives
    C.  Mayans
    D.  Ship

6. What can be inferred from paragraph 4 about Cortez's discovery of the cocoa beans?

    A.  He was probably disappointed.
    B.  He was excited.
    C.  He was elated about the discovery.
    D.  He was saddened.

7. Select the TWO answer choices that are mentioned in paragraph 5 as being reasons chocolate became popular in the 1500s. *To receive credit, you must select TWO answers.*

    A.  The nuns flavor the chocolate drink with vanilla.
    B.  The nuns made the drink more popular to Europeans.
    C.  The European palate was more refined.
    D.  The drink had added sugar.

8. The word 'monopoly' in paragraph 6 is closest in meaning to

    A. exclusive control
    B. right to sell in large quantities
    C. ability to exploit the market
    D. cartel

9. Select TWO answer choices mentioned in paragraph 8 as being reasons the hydraulic press improved the processing of chocolate. To receive credit, you must select TWO answers.

   A. It could eliminate most of the chocolate.
   B. It could eliminate most of the fat.
   C. It could use the remains of the paste.
   D. It could grind the beans into powder.

10. **In paragraph 8, there is a missing sentence. The paragraph is repeated below and show four letters (A, B, C, and D) that indicate where the following sentence could be added.**

**Van Houten also discovered how to neutralize the acidity of the product by using potash.**

Many attempts were made to eliminate the bitterness and oiliness by adding wheat, corn or oat flour. **(A)** Nothing worked until Coenraad van Houten invented a hydraulic press that could extract two thirds of the fat. The press had two great advantages. **(B)** It could eliminate most of the fat which could be used to make chocolate for eating, and it could use the remains of the paste for grinding into cocoa powder. **(C)** The alkalizing process, called *dutching*, allowed the powder to remain suspended in liquids for longer periods of time. **(D)**

   A. Option A
   B. Option B
   C. Option C
   D. Option D

11. The word 'confections' in paragraph 10 is closest in meaning to

   A. cakes
   B. candy
   C. desserts
   D. any type of sweet preparation

12. In paragraph 10, which one of the following is **NOT** mentioned as a major statistic about chocolate?

   A. Worldwide chocolate consumption was 7.3 million tons in 2015-2016.
   B. Milk chocolate accounted for over 50% of the total consumption.
   C. The Swiss eat the most chocolate.
   D. The United States prefers milk chocolate to other types of chocolate.

13. In paragraph 11, all of the following statements are mentioned EXCEPT

    A. 2/3 of the cocoa production comes from Central America.
    B. Barry Callehaut is the largest b2b chocolate company in the world.
    C. Callehaut sells about 42% of their products to Europe.
    D. Callehaut sells about 1.8 million tonnes to Europe and America annually.

14. Directions: An introductory sentence for a brief summary of the passage is provided below. Complete the summary by selecting the THREE answer choices that express the most important ideas in the passage. Some sentences do not belong in the summary because they express ideas that are not presented in the passage or are minor ideas in the passage. *This question is worth 2 points.*

Write your answer choices in the spaces where they belong. You can either write the letter of your answer choice or you can copy the sentence.

| Chocolate has grown in popularity over the years, but at first, it was not popular in Europe. |
| --- |
| • |
| • |
| • |

    A. Chocolate was first discovered in the Americas about 2500 years ago.
    B. Columbus and King Ferdinand V did not like chocolate at first.
    C. Because of nun in the Guanaco convent, chocolate became more popular.
    D. Today, chocolate is a billion dollar industry.
    E. The hydraulic press extracted 2/3 of the fat making modern chocolate possible.
    F. Cortez had a more important role in the popularization of chocolate than Columbus.

| | The African Violet |
|---|---|
| 1 | The history of the African violet is one where a species from Africa took the world by storm for many reasons. The violet was discovered in 1892 in the Usambara Mountains in Tanganyika (now Tanzania) by Baron Walter von Saint Paul. He sent seeds and maybe some plants to his father in Germany. The Director of the Royal Botanic Garden declared them a new **species**. |
| 2 | The plant was named *Saintpaulia ionantlia*. The *Saintpaulia* was to honor the discoverer of the plants. The Greek word ***ionantha*** means with violet like flowers. Many years later, another botanist discovered that there were actually two species in the plants sent to Germany by Baron von Saint Paul. This second species was named *Saintpaulia confusa*. |
| 3 | In 1893, the first African violets were shipped to a New York from Europe. Years later, the Armacost and Royston Nursery in Los Angeles obtained seeds from Germany and England. From their seedlings, the nursery selected ten plants became known as the original ten. These ten seedlings and two species plants have produced most of the over 18,000 registered plants in existence today through **hybridizing**. |
| 4 | Over the years, several more species plants were added to the original classification of the *Saintpaulia* and increased the known varieties to more than twenty. They were later reduced to six. However, modern DNA testing has entered the **fray** and in 2015, the species were listed as ten. Scientists studied their leaf structure, geographical location in the wild and their evolutionary development. |
| 5 | The work of scientists in classifying African violets might seem **frivolous** at first, but the plants are extremely valuable commercially. The information the scientific community gives commercial growers, who are constantly creating new hybrids, contributes to the violet's commercial success. In 2015, the potted flowering plants were valued at $714 million with California and Florida being the two biggest growers. While this figure is reflective of all flowering indoor plants, African violets were a major player in this market. Commercial growers like African violets because they can produce a flowering plant in five to six weeks and because of the huge variety of plants. The African violet is called "America's favorite houseplant" for a reason! |
| | |
| | Sources: Bartholomew, P. and AVSA. Growing to Show. Rev. 2008. Waterloo, Iowa. Pioneer graphics, 119 p.. <br> Nishii, K. et al Streptocarpus redefined to include all Afro-Malagasy Gesneriaceae:… Taxon 64 (6) December 2015: 1243-1274. <br> USAD. Floriculture Crops. 2015 Summary. |

15. The word 'species' in paragraph 1 is closest in meaning to
    A. Plant
    B. A distinct kind
    C. Different color
    D. Flowering plant

16. Where does the word *ionantha* in paragraph 2come from

    A. Greek
    B. Germany
    C. Africa
    D. Europe

17. How did the African violet get the name *Saintpaulia*?

    A. From the native African culture.
    B. From the Greek
    C. From the last name of the discoverer
    D. From the Tanganyika language

18. The word 'hybridizing' in paragraph 3 is closest in meaning to

    A. Crossbreeding
    B. Mixing
    C. Purifying
    D. Detoxifying

19. The word 'fray' in paragraph 4 is closest in meaning to

    A. Discussion
    B. Talks
    C. Conversation
    D. Brawl

20. According to paragraph 4, how did scientists determine the current number of species? *Choose 2 answers.*

    A. By studying taxonomy charts
    B. By studying the DNA of the plants
    C. By studying their geographical location in the wild
    D. By looking at plants and their characteristics

21. Why is the scientific classification of the *Saintpaulia* important?

    A. It is an important commercial product.
    B. There is a huge number of varieties.
    C. Scientific knowledge satisfies our curiosity.
    D. The plants are easy to grow.

22. Write the letter or the sentence of the THREE (3) best answer choices that express the most important ideas of the passage. **This question is worth 2 points.**

| **The African violet is America's favorite houseplant for many reasons.** |
|---|
| • |
| • |
| • |

Choose 3 answers from the following choices.

1. African violets have many different hybrids.

2. African violets are a huge commercial success.

3. African violets are easy to grow.

4. Commercial growers can produce a crop in 5-6 weeks.

5. There are many more species that originally thought.

6. Flowering indoor plants, including African violets, are a huge economic market.

**Part 3_b**

**Reading Comprehension**

Directions: Read the passage. Then answer the questions that follow the passage.

|   | MOUNTAINS |
|---|---|
| 1 | Mountains are all around us on the surface of the Earth and in the ocean's depths. They are caused by different types of movement of the Earth. Many mountains exist on each of the continents, but what are mountains? Geologists classify land masses of higher than 1,000 feet as mountains, and mountain close together as chains or mountain ranges. |
| 2 | Mountains often **function** as the boundaries between different countries (like the Pyrenees that separate Spain and Portugal) or mountains can act as a protective barrier that protect countries from invading armies. Switzerland has used their natural landscape to prevent invasions and to provide refuge for centuries.  Because of the high Alps, Switzerland has remained neutral for most of its existence. |
| 3 | There are four main types of mountains: fault-block mountains (such as the Sierra Nevada in California), volcanic mountains (such as Mount St. Helens in Washington State), dome mountains (such as the Black Hills of South Dakota), and plateau mountains (such as mountains in New Zealand). |
| 4 | Simply explained, plate tectonics cause gigantic pieces of the Earth's crust to fold and **buckle** or break into blocks.  Volcanic and fault-block mountains form when the plates collide with each other. The crust (also called lithosphere) 'floats' on the surface of the Earth. Beneath the lithosphere lies the asthenosphere, a layer of solid rock that **is subjected to** so much heat and pressure that is becomes liquid. If the asthenosphere pushes through the cracks and rises, it causes fault-block mountains.  If the crust breaks into gigantic blocks; the blocks can move up and down and may stack on top of each other. |
| 5 | **Dome** mountains are formed when the magma rises up but doesn't break through the surface of the Earth's crust. As the dome hardens, it remains higher than the surrounding area and is worn away by wind and rain erosion.  The mountains become more circular and have rounded tops. |
| 6 | Plateau mountains are formed in a way similar to dome mountains. The tectonic plates push up huge chunks of land, but without folding or faulting. These mountains are then formed by other elements such as erosion or **weathering**. |
| 7 | Mountains impact our lives and play. They affect our weather, the flow of water, and animal and plant life. When mountains are formed by volcanic eruptions, minerals are brought to the surface. Because many rivers begin in the high mountain peaks, mountains are good place to build electric power stations. Mountains provide the **site** for many winter sports, such as skiing and snowboarding. Since man cannot move mountains, he has learned to live with nature's landscape. |
| SOURCES | Barrow, M. The Mountain Environment. http://www.primaryhomeworkhelp.co.uk/mountains/types.htm |

| | Mountains: highest points on Earth. http://science.nationalgeographic.com/science/earth/surface-of-the-earth/mountains-article |
|---|---|

23. This passage is mainly about

    A. How mountains are made
    B. Description of the different types of mountains
    C. How mountains function
    D. Description of mountains and their functions

24. The word 'function' in paragraph 2 is closest in meaning to

    A. Act
    B. Goal
    C. Work
    D. Power

25. In paragraph 2, all of the following are given as reasons mountains protect humans EXCEPT

    A. To establish borders between countries
    B. To deter enemies
    C. To provide recreation
    D. To prevent invading armies

26. What can be inferred from the information in paragraphs 2 and 3 about mountains?

    A. Mountains are prevalent on Earth.
    B. Mountains are rare on the Earth's surface.
    C. Different types of mountains are formed in different locations on Earth.
    D. The Alps are domed mountains.

27. The word 'buckle' in paragraph 4 is closest in meaning to

    A. Yield
    B. Knuckle
    C. Bend
    D. Clasp

28. The words 'is subjected to' in paragraph 4 are closest in meaning to

    A. Is removed from
    B. Undergoes
    C. Is vulnerable to
    D. Experiences

29. What is plate tectonics?

    A. Blocks of Earth that move
    B. Movement of pieces of the Earth's crust
    C. Explanation of how mountains are formed
    D. Volcanoes that form mountains

30. Which of the following can be inferred from the description of plate tectonics in paragraph 4?

    A. Volcanic and fault-block mountains are formed in the same way.
    B. Any amount of force can cause a plate to collide with another plate
    C. Plates exist in only a few countries.
    D. The surface of the Earth is in constant motion.

31. The word 'dome' in paragraph 5 is closest in meaning to

    A. Cupola
    B. Oval
    C. Ragged
    D. peaked

32. The word 'weathering' in paragraph 6 is closest in meaning to

    A. effects of natural elements on a mountain
    B. physical effects on land surfaces
    C. chemical effects on mountains
    D. changed by rain

33. The word 'site' in paragraph 7 is closest in meaning to

    A. sitting room
    B. place
    C. resort
    D. land

34. In paragraph 7 of the passage, a sentence is missing. Look at the paragraph, which is repeated below, and choose one of the four letters (A, B, C, and D) to indicate where the following sentence could be added.

**Because many rivers begin in the high mountain peaks, mountains are good place to build electric power stations.**

Mountains impact our lives and play. They affect our weather, the flow of water, and animal and plant life. (A)  When mountains are formed by volcanic eruptions, minerals are brought to the surface. (B) Mountains provide the **site** for many winter sports, such as skiing and snowboarding. (C) Since man cannot move mountains, he has learned to live with nature's landscape.  (D)

    A. Option A
    B. Option B
    C. Option C
    D. Option D

35. **Directions: In the following table, a sentence is provided to introduce a summary of the passage. Choose THREE more sentences from the sentences below to complete your summary. Some of the sentences given are not included in the passage or are minor ideas from the passage.** *The question is worth 2 points.*

Write your answers in the space below. You can just write the letter of the sentence or copy the whole sentence.

| Mountains are formed by powerful geological forces and mankind has learned how to use them to his advantage. |
|---|
| • |
| • |
| • |

Answer Choices

A. Mountains have many functions in the development of different countries.

B. Plate tectonics can be used to explain how mountains are formed.

C. Dome mountains are formed by magma.

D. Weathering shapes plateau mountains.

E. Mountains determine how we work and many of our sports.

F. Natural forces shape the Earth.

Directions: Read the passage. Then answer the questions that follow the passage.

| 1 | Positive psychology is a relatively new branch of psychology. It can be defined as the scientific study of happiness or as the study of the strengths that enable people and communities to succeed. Positive psychology tries to explain and understand happiness and well-being. Throughout history, mankind has looked for explanations for these human **traits.** Socrates said, "The secret of change is to focus all of your energy, not on fighting the old, but on building the new." He believed in knowing oneself. |
|---|---|
| 2 | Despite the long history of happiness, psychologists dwelt on digging into people's pasts, **ferreting out** their secrets, and analyzing minute details of their pasts. Positive psychology is just the opposite. It emphasizes the importance building on the positive aspects of people's lives and helping them enjoy their present and having hope for a happy future. |
| 3 | Positive psychology was first proposed in 1998 by Martin Seligman, a University of Pennsylvania psychologist. In his address to the American Psychological Association, he started a new movement in psychology by **exhorting** his fellow psychologists to "turn toward understanding and building the human strengths to complement our emphasis on healing damage." In his book *Flourish: A Visionary New Understanding of Happiness and Well-being (2011)*, Seligman expanded his theory to include positive relationships and accomplishments. |
| 4 | Positive psychology has since focused on three areas of human **endeavor**: positive emotions, positive individual traits and positive institutions. To develop positive emotions, people must be content with their past, happy in the present and hopeful for the future. The individual's positive traits come from his or her individual strengths and virtues. Positive institutions focus on how to improve a community by utilizing its strengths. |
| 5 | We don't need to be happy or joyful all the time. Happiness is not a response to dangerous situations. We need a range of emotions to help protect us from dangerous—fight or flight—situations. We need happiness and joy to compensate for the negative emotions in order to live a positive life as we **seek** happiness. Joy is the ultimate response that we can experience, but we can't sustain it for long. Joy is **fleeting**. |
| 6 | Another key to positive change is positive relationships. Married couples are happier than single people. Researchers debate the reasons why, but the fact remains that happily married couples live longer, have better social skills, and are healthier. |
| 7 | Strong and healthy social ties are another key to positive living. The Framingham Heart Study found that happiness and unhappiness tended to spread through close relationships. Researchers found that happiness spread more consistently than unhappiness through the network. Having a good friend helps people **cushion** the impact of negative life experiences, and thus, increases one's self-esteem. Social interactions, such as a gift of flowers, may affect a wide variety of emotions. |
| 8 | Age does matter. Researchers have shown that during their 20s and 70s, individuals are happier than during the decades of the 40s and 50s. The reasons are not entirely clear, but some facts stand out. After the 20s, feelings of stress and anger decline. Perhaps it is because certain social skills take time to develop or perhaps it is because hormones become more stabilized. Older people have more health problems, but fewer problems in general. |
| 9 | Money cannot buy happiness according to the old **saying**. Research seems to support this |

| | |
|---|---|
| | adage. Money is important to the poor who have not met their basic needs, but less so to the middle class and the wealthy. Lottery winners have higher levels of happiness immediately after winning, but the happiness level soon drops and returns to previous levels within a short period of time. |
| 10 | Personality plays an important part in our happiness. **Genetics** play a role in our personality and the emotions associated with personality. Neuroscientists believe that genetics control approximately 80% of our long-term sense of well-being leaving 20% that can be influenced by the environment and learning from sources such as positive change. |
| 11 | Many researchers believe that individual differences are important, but research to date suggests that most people will benefit from the **doctrines** of Positive Psychology. Psychologists will continue to develop new techniques and exercises to improve our daily lives, and this is good. All human experience moves forward by experimenting, discarding the things that don't work well and accepting new challenges. |

36.  What is the main idea of the passage?

    A.  Positive Psychology is good for us.
    B.  Positive Psychology is a new field.
    C.  What is Positive Psychology?
    D.  An explanation of Seligman's theory.


37. The word 'traits' in paragraph 1 is closest in meaning to

    A.  Quantity
    B.  Individual
    C.  Quality
    D.  Ideology


38. The words 'ferreting out' in paragraph 2 is closest in meaning to

    A. secreting
    B. searching for
    C. disguising
    D. suppressing

39. The word 'exhorted' in paragraph 3 is closest in meaning to

   A. Impeded
   B. Absolved
   C. Deterred
   D. Urged

40. All of the following are mentioned in paragraph 4 as elements of Positive Psychology EXCEPT

   A. Positive emotions
   B. Positive institutions
   C. Positive communities
   D. Positive individual traits

41. The word 'fleeting' in paragraph 5 is closest in meaning to

   A. Short-lived
   B. Persistent
   C. Lasting
   D. Enduring

42. The word 'cushion' in paragraph 7 is closest in meaning to

   A. Harden
   B. An object to sit on
   C. Absorb
   D. Encircle

43. Which of the following is NOT mentioned in paragraph 7 as a reason that social ties are important?

   A.  Good friends lessen the impact of negative life experiences.
   B. Good friends increase a person's self-esteem.
   C. Social interactions may affect a wide variety of emotions.
   D. Happiness is easier to spread than unhappiness in social networks.

44. All of the following are mentioned in paragraph 8 as reasons why age matters in happiness EXCEPT

    A. Hormones settle down after the 20s.
    B. Older people have fewer problems in general.
    C. Older people don't have problems getting around.
    D. Stress and anger decline in the 20s.

45. The word 'saying' in paragraph 9 is closest in meaning to

    A. Talking
    B. Sawyer
    C. Spreading
    D. Proverb

46. What can be inferred from paragraph 9 about money and happiness?

    A. Money can't buy happiness.
    B. The poor are happier.
    C. The middle class have their basic needs met.
    D. The wealthy are very happy.

47. The word 'genetics' in paragraph 10 is closest in meaning to

    A. Branch of biology
    B. Study of history
    C. Family
    D. Relatives

48. The word 'doctrines' in paragraph 11 is closest in meaning to

    A. Evidence
    B. Documentation
    C. Stubborn
    D. Dogmas

49. In paragraph 10, a sentence has been left out. The paragraph is repeated below and shows four letters (A, B, C, D) that indicate where the sentence below could be added.

**Extroverts seem to be happier and perhaps this is because they develop stronger relationships and have more support groups than introverts.**

**(A)** Personality plays an important part in our happiness. **(B)** <u>Genetics</u> play a role in our personality and the emotions associated with personality. **(C)** Neuroscientists believe that genetics control approximately 80% of our long-term sense of well-being leaving 20% that can be influenced by the environment and learning from sources such as positive change. **(D)**

    A. Option A
    B. Option B
    C. Option C
    D. Option D

50. Directions: An beginning sentence for a short summary of the passage is given below. Complete the summary by choosing THREE answer choices that express the most important ideas in the passage. Some of the sentences may present ideas not presented in the passage or are minor details. *This question is worth 2 points.*

You may write the letter of your choice or you can copy your sentence in the spaces below.

| **Positive Psychology is a new branch of psychology.** |
| --- |
| • |
| • |
| • |

Answer Choices

A. According to Positive Psychology, we can determine our own happiness.

B. Positive Psychology has focused on three areas of human endeavor.

C. Positive Psychology was the brain-child of an unknown psychologist.

D. We don't have to be happy all the time.

E. Factors, such as health, wealth, and social status, are important in our happiness level.

F. Money, age, and personality are factors that are an important part of our happiness.

# Writing Practice Test

# Writing Section Practice Test

## TASK 1:

You have just leased a new car in an English-speaking country. The car has not been starting properly, which has caused you to be late for work multiple times.

Write a letter to the manager of the car dealership. The manager's name is Mr. Smith. In your letter:

- Introduce yourself
- Explain the nature of the problem
- Request what you would like the manager to do to fix the problem.

Dear Mr. Smith,

_____

_____

_____

_____

_____

_____

_____

_____

_____

_____

_____

_____

_____

_____

_____

_____

## TASK 2:

Respond to the following prompt using at least 250 words.  Use examples from your experience or knowledge you have to support your opinion.

Prompt:

*More than ever, people today use smart-phone apps to accomplish normal tasks by paying other people. This includes grocery shopping and other small tasks such as picking up clothes from the dry-cleaner.*

*Do you think this is a positive trend?  Explain why or why not using examples.*

Use the following 2 pages, as needed, to complete your response..

# Listening Answers

# LISTENING ANSWER KEY

The correct answers for multiple choice are **highlighted in bold** as are the fill in the blank answers. The questions requiring you to write an answer in a certain number of words or fewer will have a bullet list of examples of acceptable answers.

## RECORDING #1 ANSWER KEY

1. *Fill in the blank to complete this sentence:*

   The female speakers mother went to a **convention** last week.

2. Where was the speaker's mother last week?
   a. Arizona
   **b. Albuquerque**
   c. Alabama
   d. Utah

3. The speaker's mother complained of pain in her:
   **a. Knees**
   b. Back
   c. Hands
   d. Shoulders

4. The female speaker stated that her mother is usually very healthy.
   **a. True**
   b. False

5. Her mother had to climb up and down a lot of:
   a. Ramps
   **b. Stairs**
   c. Escalators
   d. Uneven sidewalks

6. What was the mother's difficulty with attending the presentations?
   a. She could not find the correct room.
   b. She had difficulty hearing the speakers.
   c. She was late because her watch broke.
   **d. Going up and down stairs hurt her knees.**

7. *Fill in the blank to complete this sentence:*

   The male speaker says he is from **Mexico City**.

8. The male speaker says the altitude is over _____ feet high where he is from.
   a. 1,000
   b. 2,000
   c. 3,000
   **d. 7,000**

9. When tourists get altitude sickness, all of the following happen EXCEPT
   a. It usually lasts several days.
   b. It causes breathing problems.
   c. They feel a little sick.
   **d. They pass out and lose consciousness.**

10. According to the male speaker, altitude sickness usually passes in a few _____.
    a. Weeks
    b. Hours
    c. Minutes
    **d. Days**

## Recording #2 Answer Key

11. At the beginning of recording, where did the speaker say he has backpacked before?
    a. **Europe**
    b. Uruguay
    c. Uganda
    d. East Asia

12. The speaker indicated he enjoys traveling alone because of which of the following:
    a. **It encourages him to communicate with the local people**
    b. It is less expensive
    c. He does not enjoy being with other travelers
    d. He is traveling for work and must focus

13. In 4 or fewer words, describe where would the speaker write his observations in his notebook?

    *Examples of acceptable answers:*
    - *Café*
    - *Restaurant*
    - *Small café*
    - *Small restaurant*
    - *Small restaurant or cafe*

14. True or False: the speaker would often forget to write in his notebook as he spent more time talking to the other diners?
    a. **True**
    b. False

15. In 3 or fewer words, describe one drawback of traveling alone that the speaker mentioned.

    *Examples of acceptable answers:*
    - *It is expensive*
    - *It is lonely*
    - *Lonely and expensive*

16. Based on your interpretation of everything the speaker said, which of the following is an opinion he is most likely to share:
    a. It is dangerous to travel alone, so only experienced travelers should try it.
    b. Traveling with a group is more fun, but if no one else wants to go, traveling alone is OK.
    **c. You should try traveling alone because you have a different opportunity to meet new people.**
    d. Traveling alone is only fun if you backpack by yourself.

17. The speaker said that in the future, he intends to backpack travel to:
    a. Egypt
    b. Europe
    c. South America
    **d. None of the above**

18. Based on your interpretation of the opinions expressed by the speaker, which of the following is the holiday or vacation he would most likely choose?
    a. A cruise ship from his own country
    b. A luxury hotel resort vacation with family
    c. A trip to a foreign country he has visited before
    **d. A trip to a new foreign country alone**

19. True or False: The speaker thinks it is great to travel alone, except that he would prefer to have a group so he did not have to make decisions alone.
    a. True
    **b. False**

20. *Fill in the blank to complete the sentence below:*

    The speaker said that it is more **expensive** to stay in a hotel room by yourself.

## RECORDING #3 ANSWER KEY

21. What are the speakers mainly discussing?
    a.   How the woman should prepare for her class.
    b.   The woman's responsibilities at home.
    c.   The plans to widen the highway near the school.
    d.   **Different events of everyday life.**

22. Who is difficult for the female speaker to please?
    a.   The male speaker
    b.   **Her boss**
    c.   Her parents
    d.   Her mom

*#23 & #24: use the below question to answer both questions #23 and #24.*

Why does the male speaker believe that the widening of the highway will cause difficulties for him to get to school?

*(Note for answer key: Answering either A or D is acceptable in any order, as long as you selected only one each for 23 and 24).*

23. Choose one correct answer below:
    a.   **The roads will be narrower.**
    b.   There will be more traffic.
    c.   There will be many bicycles on the roads.
    d.   There will be fewer exits.

24. Choose the 2nd correct answer below:
    a.   The roads will be narrower.
    b.   There will be more traffic.
    c.   There will be many bicycles on the roads.
    d.   **There will be fewer exits.**

25. What does the male student mean when he says: *"on the dot at 10"*?
    a. The test begins around 10.
    **b. The test begins precisely at 10.**
    c. The test will start as soon as the students arrive for their 10 class.
    d. The test at approximately 10 o'clock.

26. Why does the man mean when he says: 'we will have to get up earlier and leave home earlier'?
    a. It will take him longer to travel to school because of traffic police.
    b. The roads will be more congested because of more exits.
    c. He expects the next year's classes to begin earlier.
    **d. The man thinks construction will cause traffic delays.**

27. According to the recording, what is flan?
    a. A cooked banana.
    b. An appetizer.
    **c. A dessert.**
    d. Heaven in your mouth

28. What does the man's favorite sport?
    a. Soccer
    b. Football
    **c. Cycling**
    d. Basketball

29. Why does the woman find it difficult to do her job at the restaurant well?
    a. Because her boss is very demanding.
    b. Because she has a poor memory.
    c. Because the boss is always complaining.
    **d. Because they get very busy at times.**

30. *Fill in the blank to complete the following sentence:*

The female speaker said that her family's favorite food is beans and rice, and they come from the country of **Columbia**.

# Recording #4 ANSWER KEY

1. What is the lecture mainly about?
    a. **Innovations in nanotechnology**
    b. A comparison of nanotechnology and previous technology.
    c. The ethics of nanotechnology
    d. Problems with nanotechnology.

2. In what way is nanotechnology different from previous technology?
    a. It is smaller.
    b. **It is microscopic.**
    c. It is larger.
    d. It is huge.

3. According to the professor, which one of the following options is an actual nanotechnology product in use today?
    a. Clothing that can wash itself.
    b. Bandages that kill bacteria by eliminating their food source.
    c. Scratch-proof paint for cars.
    d. **Glass that can clean itself.**

4. In his next class, the professor will lecture about all of the following EXCEPT
    a. Creating a new race of humans
    b. The economics of nanotechnology
    c. The ethics of more lethal weapons
    d. **The need for smaller medical devices**

5. *Fill in the blank to complete the following sentence.*

    A probe is being used in cardiology centers around the world to get images from inside a patient's **arteries**.

6. According to the professor, the layer of Zinc-Oxide protects against what?
    a. Coffee stains
    b. Blood stains
    **c. UV radiation**
    d. Bleach


7. True or False: While a tennis racket with nano-tube infused graphite is very light, but is not as strong as traditional steel or aluminum rackets.
    a. True
    **b. False**


8. *Fill in the blank to complete the following sentence:*

    Some scientists believe that nanoparticles could be dangerous to humans because they could pass from the bloodstream to the **brain**.


9. True or False: An advantage that helps scientists is that on a nano-scale, atoms in larger groups act very similarly as they do in small groups.
    a. True
    **b. False**


10. The tennis ball created by Wilson has a double core, one of which is made of _____ nanoparticles:
    a. Rubber
    b. Titanium
    **c. Clay**
    d. Graphite

# Reading Answers

## Part 3

## Reading Comprehension

Directions: Read the passage. Then answer the questions.

| 1 | No one knows exactly how chocolate was discovered. Approximately, one thousand years ago, somewhere in Central America, the Mayan Indians began to roast the odd shaped fruit and use the seeds in a drink called *chocolatl* or *xocoatl*. This "bitter water" has evolved into what we know today as hot chocolate. |
|---|---|
| 2 | Historians believe that the way to use and enjoy the cocoa fruit was discovered over 2500 years ago. The fruit was probably used for the pulp which was slightly acidic. Later the beans or seeds were roasted and **pulverized** to make a thick, **coarse** paste. This paste was flavored with different seeds, vanilla, chilies and honey.  After the paste was flavored, it was allowed to dry. The chocolate paste became hard and could easily be transported by the natives in rectangular shapes called tablets. The natives used the chocolate tablets to make a drink by dissolving the tablets in water and whipping it until frothy. |
| 3 | Columbus discovered chocolate on his fourth trip to the Americas. He did not like the drink as prepared by the natives. Yet, he realized the beans were valuable to the Mayans because they rushed to pick up some beans that fell when the Spaniards were loading their ship with **them**. He carried some beans back to King Ferdinand V of Spain who was not impressed with them at first. |
| 4 | Hernan Cortez discovered also the value of the cocoa beans when he found Moctezuma's treasury. He had expected to find gold, but instead he found more than one billion cocoa beans. The Spaniard realized they were valuable, but he wasn't sure exactly how. |
| 5 | Cortez learned how to prepare chocolate and carried his knowledge back to Spain where it remained unpopular.  In 1530 and 1540, the nuns at the Guanaco convent in South America began adding sugar and vanilla to the drink. This made the drink more popular to the European palate. |
| 6 |  For almost 100 years, Spain and her colonies maintained a **monopoly** on the cocoa beans. In 1606, the monopoly ended and other European nations began to obtain the cocoa beans and produce chocolate. |
| 7 | The cocoa beverage became very popular in Europe through the royal courts and the nobility. Chocolate houses were the rage, yet the drink would probably not appeal to us today. The drink was thick, acrid, and greasy. |
| 8 | Many attempts were made to eliminate the bitterness and oiliness by adding wheat, corn or oat flour. Nothing worked until Coenraad van Houten invented a hydraulic press that could extract two thirds of the fat. The press had two great advantages. It could eliminate most of the fat which could be used to make chocolate for eating, and it could use the remains of the paste for grinding into cocoa powder.  The alkalizing process, called *dutching*, allowed the powder to remain suspended in liquids for longer periods of time. |
| 9 | The manufacture of modern chocolate candy began over 150 years ago in Sweden by the Swiss brothers Cloetta who built their Steam-Chocolate-Factory in the city of Malmo. When |

| | |
|---|---|
| | another Swiss discovered how to manufacture milk solids, the milk chocolate candy bar was created. |
| 10 | In modern times, chocolate **confections** became a billion dollar industry. The world's biggest consumer of chocolate is Switzerland with an average of 19.8 pounds per person followed by Germany at 17.4 pounds. The United States comes in ninth on this chart with only 9.5 pounds per person. According to Statista in 2016, worldwide chocolate confectionery consumption was a staggering 7.3 million tons in 2015-2016. Milk chocolate is the preferred flavor with over 50% of the market. |
| 11 | Even though cocoa beans were discovered in the Americas, more than two-thirds of the world's production comes from West Africa. The largest company in the world that manufactures and sells chocolate and cocoa products is Barry Callebaut. This wholesaler, a business-to-business (b2b) entity, produces chocolate that appears in one of five products around the world. About 42% and 26% of their chocolate products are sold to Europe and America respectively of an astonishing 1.8 million tonnes. |
| | |
| | |
| Sources | Young, A.M. The chocolate tree—a natural history of chocolate. Washington: Smithsonian Institute Press.<br>Barry Callebaut website: https://www.barry-callebaut.com/at-a-glance |

Directions: Answer the following questions.

1. The word "pulverized" in paragraph 2 is closest in meaning to

    A.  carefully preserved

    B.  decimated

    C.  destroyed

    D.  crushed

Answer: D. Crushed
The correct word choice is crushed (pressed or pounded) into a powder or dust.

2. The word "coarse" in paragraph 2 is closest in meaning to

    A. rough

    B. consisting of large particles

    C. fine or delicate

    D. uneven

Answer: B. consisting of large particles
The correct word choice is 'consisting of large particles' the opposite of fine or delicate.

3. Which of the following made the tablets easy to transport?

    A. The tablets were hard and dry.
    B. The tablets were stackable.
    C. The tablets were small.
    D. The tablets were easily broken.

Answer: A. The tablets were hard and dry.
According to the paragraph 2, the tablets were hard and dry. The other factors were not mentioned in the text.

4. What can be inferred from paragraph 1 and 2 as reasons King Ferdinand V did not like the chocolate drink?

    A. The drink was not well prepared
    B. His friends did not like the drink either.
    C. The drink was bitter.
    D. The flavors were unusual.

Answer: C. The drink was bitter.
In paragraph 1, the drink was referred to as 'bitter water'. Even though the paste was 'flavored' with honey, apparently it still wasn't a sweet drink because it would probably not turn hard and dry if it had a lot of honey in the mixture.

5. What does the word them in paragraph 3 refer to?

    A. Beans
    B. Natives
    C. Mayans
    D. Ship

Answer: A. beans
The word 'them' refers back to the word 'beans', its antecedent even though there are many other nouns between the words them and beans.

6. What can be inferred from paragraph 4 about Cortez's discovery of the cocoa beans?

    A. He was probably disappointed.
    B. He was excited.
    C. He was elated about the discovery.
    D. He was saddened.

Answer: A. He was probably disappointed.
Cortez was expecting to find gold when he discovered Moctezuma's treasury. Gold was a known valuable element, but the value of cocoa beans was unknown. Cortez didn't not know why the natives valued these beans so much.

7. Select the TWO answer choices that are mentioned in paragraph 5 as being reasons chocolate became popular in the 1500s. *To receive credit, you must select TWO answers.*

    A. The nuns flavor the chocolate drink with vanilla.
    B. The nuns made the drink more popular to Europeans.
    C. The European palate was more refined.
    D. The drink had added sugar.

Answers: A. The nuns flavored the chocolate drink with vanilla <u>AND</u> D. The drink had added sugar.
The answers B and C are true statements but are not reasons the drink became more popular. A and D are the correct answer choices.

8. The word 'monopoly' in paragraph 6 is closest in meaning to

    A. exclusive control
    B. right to sell in large quantities
    C. ability to exploit the market
    D. cartel

Answer: A. exclusive control
The word 'monopoly' is closets in meaning to A. exclusive control.

9. Select TWO answer choices mentioned in paragraph 8 as being reasons the hydraulic press improved the processing of chocolate. To receive credit, you must select TWO answers.

    A. It could eliminate most of the chocolate.
    B. It could eliminate most of the fat.
    C. It could use the remains of the paste.
    D. It could grind the beans into powder.

Answers: B. It could eliminate most of the fat AND C. It could use the remains of the paste. Paragraph 8 clearly states the reasons given in B and C. Answer A is the opposite of Answer B. Answer D mentions grinding whereas the hydraulic press means to apply steady force or weight.

10. **In paragraph 8, there is a missing sentence. The paragraph is repeated below and show four letters (A, B, C, and D) that indicate where the following sentence could be added.**

**Van Houten also discovered how to neutralize the acidity of the product by using potash.**

Many attempts were made to eliminate the bitterness and oiliness by adding wheat, corn or oat flour. **(A)** Nothing worked until Coenraad van Houten invented a hydraulic press that could extract two thirds of the fat. The press had two great advantages. **(B)** It could eliminate most of the fat which could be used to make chocolate for eating, and it could use the remains of the paste for grinding into cocoa powder. **(C)** The alkalizing process, called *dutching,* allowed the powder to remain suspended in liquids for longer periods of time. **(D)**

    A. Option A
    B. Option B
    C. Option C
    D. Option D

Answer: Option C.
The correct placement of the sentence places van Houten's discovery of neutralizing the acidity before an explanation of the process and its name.

11. The word 'confections' in paragraph 10 is closest in meaning to

A. cakes
B. candy
C. desserts
D. any type of sweet preparation

Answer: D. any type of sweet preparation
The term 'confections' is used to refer to all preparations that use chocolate in their preparation, not just candies.

12. In paragraph 10, which one of the following is **NOT** mentioned as a major statistic about chocolate?

A. Worldwide chocolate consumption was 7.3 million tons in 2015-2016.
B. Milk chocolate accounted for over 50% of the total consumption.
C. The Swiss eat the most chocolate.
D. The United States prefers milk chocolate to other types of chocolate.

Answer: D. The United States prefers milk chocolate to other types of chocolate.
This statement may be true, but it is not substantiated by the text. All other facts are mentioned in the text.

13. In paragraph 11, all of the following statements are mentioned EXCEPT

A. 2/3 of the cocoa production comes from Central America.
B. Barry Callehaut is the largest b2b chocolate company in the world.
C. Callehaut sells about 42% of their products to Europe.
D. Callehaut sells about 1.8 million tonnes to Europe and America annually.

Answer: A. 2/3 of the cocoa production comes from Central America
According to the text, approximately 2/3 of the cocoa production comes from West Africa. Statement A is false.

14. Directions: An introductory sentence for a brief summary of the passage is provided below. Complete the summary by selecting the THREE answer choices that express the most important ideas in the passage. Some sentences do not belong in the summary because they express ideas that are not presented in the passage or are minor ideas in the passage. *This question is worth 2 points.*

Write your answer choices in the spaces where they belong. You can either write the letter of your answer choice or you can copy the sentence.

| Chocolate has grown in popularity over the years, but at first, it was not popular in Europe. |
|---|
| • |
| • |
| • |

A. Chocolate was first discovered in the Americas about 2500 years ago.

B. Columbus and King Ferdinand V did not like chocolate at first.

C. Because of nun in the Guanaco convent, chocolate became more popular.

D. Today, chocolate is a billion dollar industry.

E. The hydraulic press extracted 2/3 of the fat making modern chocolate possible.

F. Cortez had a more important role in the popularization of chocolate than Columbus.

Answer:

| Chocolate has grown in popularity over the years, but at first, it was not popular in Europe. |
| --- |
| •      A.      Chocolate was first discovered in the Americas about 2500 years ago. |
| •      E.      The hydraulic press extracted 2/3 of the fat making modern chocolate possible. |
| •      D.      Today, chocolate is a billion dollar industry. |

These three answers illustrate the different phases in the popularization of chocolate.

Directions: Read the passage. Then answer the questions.

| | The African Violet |
| --- | --- |
| 1 | The history of the African violet is one where a species from Africa took the world by storm for many reasons.  The violet was discovered in 1892 in the Usambara Mountains in Tanganyika (now Tanzania) by Baron Walter von Saint Paul. He sent seeds and maybe some plants to his father in Germany. The Director of the Royal Botanic Garden declared them a new **species**. |
| 2 | The plant was named *Saintpaulia ionantlia*. The *Saintpaulia* was to honor the discoverer of the plants. The Greek word ***ionantha*** means with violet like flowers. Many years later, another botanist discovered that there were actually two species in the plants sent to Germany by Baron von Saint Paul. This second species was named *Saintpaulia confusa*. |
| 3 | In 1893, the first African violets were shipped to a New York from Europe. Years later, the Armacost and Royston Nursery in Los Angeles obtained seeds from Germany and England.  From their seedlings, the nursery selected ten plants became known as the original ten. These ten seedlings and two species plants have produced most of the over 18,000 registered plants in existence today through **hybridizing**. |
| 4 | Over the years, several more species plants were added to the original classification of the *Saintpaulia* and increased the known varieties to more than twenty. They were later reduced to six. However, modern DNA testing has entered the **fray** and in 2015, the species were listed as ten. Scientists studied their leaf structure, geographical location in the wild and their evolutionary development. |
| 5 | The work of scientists in classifying African violets might seem **frivolous** at first, but the plants are extremely valuable commercially. The information the scientific community gives commercial growers, who are constantly creating new hybrids, contributes to the violet's commercial success. In 2015, the potted flowering plants were valued at $714 million with California and Florida being the two biggest growers. While this figure is reflective of all flowering indoor plants, African violets were |

a major player in this market. Commercial growers like African violets because they can produce a flowering plant in five to six weeks and because of the huge variety of plants. The African violet is called "America's favorite houseplant" for a reason!

Sources:  Bartholomew, P. and AVSA. Growing to Show. Rev. 2008. Waterloo, Iowa. Pioneer graphics, 119 p..
Nishii, K. et al Streptocarpus redefined to include all Afro-Malagasy Gesneriaceae:… Taxon 64 (6) December 2015: 1243-1274.
USAD. Floriculture Crops. 2015 Summary.

15.  The word 'species' in paragraph 1 is closest in meaning to
   A.  Plant
   B.  A distinct kind
   C.  Different color
   D.  Flowering plant

Answer: B. a distinct kind
Species means a distinct kind, class, sort or variety.

16. Where does the word *ionantha* in paragraph 2come from

   A.  Greek
   B.  Germany
   C.  Africa
   D.  Europe

Answer: A. Greek
The word comes from the Greek and means with violet like flowers.

17. How did the African violet get the name *Saintpaulia*?

   A.  From the native African culture.
   B.  From the Greek
   C.  From the last name of the discoverer
   D.  From the Tanganyika language

Answer: C. From the last name of the discoverer

The name of the discoverer is often used to honor the person who discovered a new animal or plant species, as in this case.

18. The word 'hybridizing' in paragraph 3 is closest in meaning to

    A.  Crossbreeding
    B.  Mixing
    C.  Purifying
    D.  Detoxifying

Answer: A. Crossbreeding
To hybridize means to cross two different species or crossbreed. The process is usually used to produce newer and better plants or animals.

19. The word 'fray' in paragraph 4 is closest in meaning to

    A.  Discussion
    B.  Talks
    C.  Conversation
    D.  Brawl

Answer:  D. Brawl
The word 'fray' indicates a brawl, that is, a noisy quarrel or fight.

20. According to paragraph 4, how did scientists determine the current number of species? *Choose 2 answers.*

    A.  By studying taxonomy charts
    B.  By studying the DNA of the plants
    C.  By studying their geographical location in the wild
    D.  By looking at plants and their characteristics

Answer: B. By studying the DNA of the plants AND C. By studying their geographical location in the wild.
According to paragraph 4, there has been many different classifications that have listed from 6 to 20 different species. The newest classification lists 10 species which scientists arrived at by testing the DNA and studying their geographical location in the wild.

21. Why is the scientific classification of the *Saintpaulia* important?

    A. It is an important commercial product.
    B. There is a huge number of varieties.
    C. Scientific knowledge satisfies our curiosity.
    D. The plants are easy to grow.

Answer: A. It is an important commercial product.
According to the text, the Saintpaulia is an important commercial product.

22. Write the letter or the sentence of the THREE (3) best answer choices that express the most important ideas of the passage. **This question is worth 2 points.**

| The African violet is America's favorite houseplant for many reasons. |
| --- |
| • |
| • |
| • |

Choose 3 answers from the following choices.
1. African violets have many different hybrids.
2. African violets are a huge commercial success.
3. African violets are easy to grow.
4. Commercial growers can produce a crop in 5-6 weeks.
5. There are many more species that originally thought.
6. Flowering indoor plants, including African violets, are a huge economic market.

Answers: 1, 2, 3
Answers 1, 2, and 3 explain why African violets popular plants.

Reading Comprehension
Questions about reading passages
**Nos. 23-50**

**Part 3_b**

**Reading Comprehension**

Directions: Read the passage. Then answer the questions that follow the passage.

|  | MOUNTAINS |
|---|---|
| 1 | Mountains are all around us on the surface of the Earth and in the ocean's depths. They are caused by different types of movement of the Earth. Many mountains exist on each of the continents, but what are mountains? Geologists classify land masses of higher than 1,000 feet as mountains, and mountain close together as chains or mountain ranges. |
| 2 | Mountains often **function** as the boundaries between different countries (like the Pyrenees that separate Spain and Portugal) or mountains can act as a protective barrier that protect countries from invading armies. Switzerland has used their natural landscape to prevent invasions and to provide refuge for centuries. Because of the high Alps, Switzerland has remained neutral for most of its existence. |
| 3 | There are four main types of mountains: fault-block mountains (such as the Sierra Nevada in California), volcanic mountains (such as Mount St. Helens in Washington State), dome mountains (such as the Black Hills of South Dakota), and plateau mountains (such as mountains in New Zealand). |
| 4 | Simply explained, plate tectonics cause gigantic pieces of the Earth's crust to fold and **buckle** or break into blocks. Volcanic and fault-block mountains form when the plates collide with each other. The crust (also called lithosphere) 'floats' on the surface of the Earth. Beneath the lithosphere lies the asthenosphere, a layer of solid rock that **is subjected to** so much heat and pressure that is becomes liquid. If the asthenosphere pushes through the cracks and rises, it causes fault-block mountains. If the crust breaks into gigantic blocks; the blocks can move up and down and may stack on top of each other. |
| 5 | **Dome** mountains are formed when the magma rises up but doesn't break through the surface of the Earth's crust. As the dome hardens, it remains higher than the surrounding area and is worn away by wind and rain erosion. The mountains become more circular and have rounded tops. |
| 6 | Plateau mountains are formed in a way similar to dome mountains. The tectonic plates push up huge chunks of land, but without folding or faulting. These mountains are then formed by other elements such as erosion or **weathering**. |
| 7 | Mountains impact our lives and play. They affect our weather, the flow of water, and animal and plant life. When mountains are formed by volcanic eruptions, minerals are brought to the surface. Because many rivers begin in the high mountain peaks, mountains are good place to build electric power stations. Mountains provide the **site** for many winter sports, such as skiing and snowboarding. Since man cannot move mountains, he has learned to live with nature's landscape. |
| SOURCES | Barrow, M. The Mountain Environment. http://www.primaryhomeworkhelp.co.uk/mountains/types.htm |

| | Mountains: highest points on Earth. http://science.nationalgeographic.com/science/earth/surface-of-the-earth/mountains-article |
|---|---|

23. This passage is mainly about

    A. How mountains are made
    B. Description of the different types of mountains
    C. How mountains function
    D. Description of mountains and their functions

Answer: D. Description of mountains and their functions

The passage describes mountains and their functions. Part of the description of mountains is how they are formed.

24. The word 'function' in paragraph 2 is closest in meaning to

    A. Act
    B. Goal
    C. Work
    D. Power

Answer: A. Act

The word function is closest in meaning to act.

25. In paragraph 2, all of the following are given as reasons mountains protect humans EXCEPT

    A. To establish borders between countries
    B. To deter enemies
    C. To provide recreation
    D. To prevent invading armies

Answer: C. To provide recreation

According to the text, mountains protect humans by providing security and borders between countries. Mountains are useful in providing recreation, but this does not protect us.

26. What can be inferred from the information in paragraphs 2 and 3 about mountains?

   A. Mountains are prevalent on Earth.
   B. Mountains are rare on the Earth's surface.
   C. Different types of mountains are formed in different locations on Earth.
   D. The Alps are domed mountains.

Answer: C. Different types of mountains are formed in different locations on Earth.
We can infer that different types of mountains are formed in different locations on Earth, because the examples used to illustrate different mountains are from different regions. The author doesn't illustrate two types of mountains with the same mountain or mountain ranges.

27. The word 'buckle' in paragraph 4 is closest in meaning to

   A. Yield
   B. Knuckle
   C. Bend
   D. Clasp

Answer: C. Bend
The word buckle, when used as a verb, means to bend.

28. The words 'is subjected to' in paragraph 4 are closest in meaning to

   A. Is removed from
   B. Undergoes
   C. Is vulnerable to
   D. Experiences

Answer: C. is vulnerable to
To subject an object or person to something suggests that they or it is vulnerable to something.

29. What is plate tectonics?

   A. Blocks of Earth that move
   B. Movement of pieces of the Earth's crust
   C. Explanation of how mountains are formed
   D. Volcanoes that form mountains

Answer: B. Movement of pieces of the Earth's crust

In its most simple form, plate tectonics is the movement of pieces of the Earth's crust.

30. Which of the following can be inferred from the description of plate tectonics in paragraph 4?

   A. Volcanic and fault-block mountains are formed in the same way.
   B. Any amount of force can cause a plate to collide with another plate
   C. Plates exist in only a few countries.
   D. The surface of the Earth is in constant motion.

Answer: D. The surface of the Earth is in constant motion.

Since the crust or lithosphere 'floats' on the surface of the Earth, we can infer that it is in constant motion because of the forces at work on the asthenosphere.

31. The word 'dome' in paragraph 5 is closest in meaning to

   A. Cupola
   B. Oval
   C. Ragged
   D. peaked

Answer: A. cupola

The word dome is closest in meaning to the architectural structure, cupola.

32. The word 'weathering' in paragraph 6 is closest in meaning to

    A. effects of natural elements on a mountain
    B. physical effects on land surfaces
    C. chemical effects on mountains
    D. changed by rain

Answer: A. effects of natural elements on a mountain
Since the passage is discussing mountains, the correct answer is a. the effects of natural elements on a mountain. This would include both the physical and chemical effects of nature.

33. The word 'site' in paragraph 7 is closest in meaning to

    A. sitting room
    B. place
    C. resort
    D. land

Answer: B. place
The word 'site' means place, location or venue.

34. In paragraph 7 of the passage, a sentence is missing. Look at the paragraph, which is repeated below, and choose one of the four letters (A, B, C, and D) to indicate where the following sentence could be added.

**Because many rivers begin in the high mountain peaks, mountains are good place to build electric power stations.**

Mountains impact our lives and play. They affect our weather, the flow of water, and animal and plant life. (A) When mountains are formed by volcanic eruptions, minerals are brought to the surface. (B) Mountains provide the **site** for many winter sports, such as skiing and snowboarding. (C) Since man cannot move mountains, he has learned to live with nature's landscape. (D)

    A. Option A
    B. Option B
    C. Option C
    D. Option D

Answer: Option B.

**35. Directions: In the following table, a sentence is provided to introduce a summary of the passage. Choose THREE more sentences from the sentences below to complete your summary. Some of the sentences given are not included in the passage or are minor ideas from the passage. *The question is worth 2 points.***

Write your answers in the space below. You can just write the letter of the sentence or copy the whole sentence.

| Mountains are formed by powerful geological forces and mankind has learned how to use them to his advantage. |
| --- |
| • |
| • |
| • |

Answer Choices

A. Mountains have many functions in the development of different countries.

B. Plate tectonics can be used to explain how mountains are formed.

C. Dome mountains are formed by magma.

D. Weathering shapes plateau mountains.

E. Mountains determine how we work and many of our sports.

F. Natural forces shape the Earth.

Answers: A, B, and E.
Sentences C and D talk about only two kinds of mountains. Sentence F talks about natural forces, but there are many natural forces not mentioned in the passage, such as gravity and magnetism of the poles.

Directions: Read the passage below. Then answer the questions that follow the passage.

| 1 | Positive psychology is a relatively new branch of psychology. It can be defined as the scientific study of happiness or as the study of the strengths that enable people and communities to succeed. Positive psychology tries to explain and understand happiness and well-being. Throughout history, mankind has looked for explanations for these human **traits.** Socrates said, "The secret of change is to focus all of your energy, not on fighting the old, but on building the new." He believed in knowing oneself. |
|---|---|
| 2 | Despite the long history of happiness, psychologists dwelt on digging into people's pasts, **ferreting out** their secrets, and analyzing minute details of their pasts. Positive psychology is just the opposite. It emphasizes the importance building on the positive aspects of people's lives and helping them enjoy their present and having hope for a happy future. |
| 3 | Positive psychology was first proposed in 1998 by Martin Seligman, a University of Pennsylvania psychologist. In his address to the American Psychological Association, he started a new movement in psychology by **exhorting** his fellow psychologists to "turn toward understanding and building the human strengths to complement our emphasis on healing damage." In his book *Flourish: A Visionary New Understanding of Happiness and Well-being (2011),* Seligman expanded his theory to include positive relationships and accomplishments. |
| 4 | Positive psychology has since focused on three areas of human **endeavor**: positive emotions, positive individual traits and positive institutions. To develop positive emotions, people must be content with their past, happy in the present and hopeful for the future. The individual's positive traits come from his or her individual strengths and virtues. Positive institutions focus on how to improve a community by utilizing its strengths. |
| 5 | We don't need to be happy or joyful all the time. Happiness is not a response to dangerous situations. We need a range of emotions to help protect us from dangerous—fight or flight—situations. We need happiness and joy to compensate for the negative emotions in order to live a positive life as we **seek** happiness. Joy is the ultimate response that we can experience, but we can't sustain it for long. Joy is **fleeting**. |
| 6 | Another key to positive change is positive relationships. Married couples are happier than single people. Researchers debate the reasons why, but the fact remains that happily married couples live longer, have better social skills, and are healthier. |
| 7 | Strong and healthy social ties are another key to positive living. The Framingham Heart Study found that happiness and unhappiness tended to spread through close relationships. Researchers found that happiness spread more consistently than unhappiness through the network. Having a good friend helps people **cushion** the impact of negative life experiences, and thus, increases one's self-esteem. Social interactions, such as a gift of flowers, may affect a wide variety of emotions. |
| 8 | Age does matter. Researchers have shown that during their 20s and 70s, individuals are happier than during the decades of the 40s and 50s. The reasons are not entirely clear, but some facts stand out. After the 20s, feelings of stress and anger decline. Perhaps it is because certain social skills take time to develop or perhaps it is because hormones become more stabilized. Older people have more health problems, but fewer problems in general. |
| 9 | Money cannot buy happiness according to the old **saying**. Research seems to support this |

| | |
|---|---|
| | adage. Money is important to the poor who have not met their basic needs, but less so to the middle class and the wealthy. Lottery winners have higher levels of happiness immediately after winning, but the happiness level soon drops and returns to previous levels within a short period of time. |
| 10 | Personality plays an important part in our happiness. **Genetics** play a role in our personality and the emotions associated with personality. Neuroscientists believe that genetics control approximately 80% of our long-term sense of well-being leaving 20% that can be influenced by the environment and learning from sources such as positive change. |
| 11 | Many researchers believe that individual differences are important, but research to date suggests that most people will benefit from the **doctrines** of Positive Psychology. Psychologists will continue to develop new techniques and exercises to improve our daily lives, and this is good. All human experience moves forward by experimenting, discarding the things that don't work well and accepting new challenges. |

36. What is the main idea of the passage?

    A. Positive Psychology is good for us.
    B. Positive Psychology is a new field.
    C. What is Positive Psychology?
    D. An explanation of Seligman's theory.

Answer: B. Positive Psychology is a new field.
The passage discusses the new field of Positive Psychology and explains some elements of the theory. It does not offer an explanation of Seligman's theory, i.e. what he said in his speech to the American Psychological Association not does it summarize what he wrote about in his book, *Flourish*.

37. The word 'traits' in paragraph 1 is closest in meaning to

    A. Quantity
    B. Individual
    C. Quality
    D. Ideology

Answer: C. quality
The word traits mean characteristic or quality.

38. The words 'ferreting out' in paragraph 2 is closest in meaning to

    A. secreting
    B. searching for
    C. disguising
    D. suppressing

Answer: B. searching for
The expression ferreting out means hunting, looking for, or searching for.

39. The word 'exhorted' in paragraph 3 is closest in meaning to

    A. Impeded
    B. Absolved
    C. Deterred
    D. Urged

Answer: D. urged
The word exhorted means to admonish strongly or to urge someone to do something.

40. All of the following are mentioned in paragraph 4 as elements of Positive Psychology EXCEPT

    A. Positive emotions
    B. Positive institutions
    C. Positive communities
    D. Positive individual traits

Answer: C. positive communities
Positive communities come from strengthening positive institutions. The words are not used as synonyms, but rather as institutions which improve communities such as a nursing home community, a school community, or a community of elder citizens.

41. The word 'fleeting' in paragraph 5 is closest in meaning to

    A. Short-lived
    B. Persistent
    C. Lasting
    D. Enduring

Answer: A. short-lived
The word fleeting means swift, rapid, or short-lived.

42. The word 'cushion' in paragraph 7 is closest in meaning to

    A. Harden
    B. An object to sit on
    C. Absorb
    D. Encircle

Answer: C. absorb
In this sentence, cushion means anything used to absorb shock, lessen the impact of something negative or that provides comfort. An examples would be steam in certain machines..

43. Which of the following is NOT mentioned in paragraph 7 as a reason that social ties are important?

    A. Good friends lessen the impact of negative life experiences.
    B. Good friends increase a person's self-esteem.
    C. Social interactions may affect a wide variety of emotions.
    D. Happiness is easier to spread than unhappiness in social networks.

Answer: B. Good friends increase a person's self-esteem.
According to paragraph 7, having good friends help people deal with negative life experiences (i.e. death, divorce, loss of a job, etc.), and therefore, dealing with these problems in a positive way increases one's self-esteem.

44. All of the following are mentioned in paragraph 8 as reasons why age matters in happiness EXCEPT

    A. Hormones settle down after the 20s.
    B. Older people have fewer problems in general.
    C. Older people don't have problems getting around.
    D. Stress and anger decline in the 20s.

Answer: C. Older people don't have problems getting around.
The paragraph discusses the reasons for different age groups becoming happier as they age. The ability of older people is lessened because some have problems moving around as they age. C is the best choice.

45. The word 'saying' in paragraph 9 is closest in meaning to

    A. Talking
    B. Sawyer
    C. Spreading
    D. Proverb

Answer: D. Proverb
A saying is a proverb or adage.

46. What can be inferred from paragraph 9 about money and happiness?

    A. Money can't buy happiness.
    B. The poor are happier.
    C. The middle class have their basic needs met.
    D. The wealthy are very happy.

Answer: C. The middle class have their basic needs met.
According to the paragraph, the middle class and the wealthy find money important, but not as much as the poor who do not have their basic needs met. Once the basic needs are met, money becomes less important to happiness.

47. The word 'genetics' in paragraph 10 is closest in meaning to

    A.  Branch of biology
    B.  Study of history
    C.  Family
    D.  Relatives

Answer: A. branch of biology
Genetics is a branch of biology that studies the origin of something.

48. The word 'doctrines' in paragraph 11 is closest in meaning to

    A.  Evidence
    B.  Documentation
    C.  Stubborn
    D.  Dogmas

Answer: D. dogmas
Doctrines mean the teachings, the beliefs, or the dogmas.

49. In paragraph 10, a sentence has been left out. The paragraph is repeated below and shows four letters (A, B, C, D) that indicate where the sentence below could be added.

**Extroverts seem to be happier and perhaps this is because they develop stronger relationships and have more support groups than introverts.**

**(A)** Personality plays an important part in our happiness. **(B)** <u>Genetics</u> play a role in our personality and the emotions associated with personality. **(C)** Neuroscientists believe that genetics control approximately 80% of our long-term sense of well-being leaving 20% that can be influenced by the environment and learning from sources such as positive change. **(D)**

    A.  Option A
    B.  Option B
    C.  Option C
    D.  Option D

Answer: B. Option B

Option B is the correct choice because the sentence is discussing a personality type—extroverts.

50. Directions: An beginning sentence for a short summary of the passage is given below. Complete the summary by choosing THREE answer choices that express the most important ideas in the passage. Some of the sentences may present ideas not presented in the passage or are minor details. *This question is worth 2 points.*

You may write the letter of your choice or you can copy your sentence in the spaces below.

| **Positive Psychology is a new branch of psychology.** |
| --- |
| • |
| • |
| • |

Answer Choices

A. According to Positive Psychology, we can determine our own happiness.

B. Positive Psychology has focused on three areas of human endeavor.

C. Positive Psychology was the brain-child of an unknown psychologist.

D. We don't have to be happy all the time.

E. Factors, such as health, wealth, and social status, are important in our happiness level.

F. Money, age, and personality are factors that are an important part of our happiness.

Answers: A, B, E.
The best choices are A, B, E.

# Writing Essay Answer

# Writing Section Practice Test - Answer Key

Dear Mr. Smith,

My name is John Rogers and I recently leased a new vehicle from your car dealership. I have experienced repeated issues with the car starting properly, which has caused me to be late for work.

I understand that my lease includes a warranty for repairs or replacement of parts in case of malfunction. I would like to schedule a time to bring my car to be checked by a mechanic to find the problem, and for it to be fixed. Since this is a new lease and the warranty covers such repairs, I believe this should be free of charge.

Please respond and let me know when I can bring my car for this work. It is important that it be done on a Saturday, because it is difficult for me to take time off from work during the week. However, I am willing to drop it off on Friday evening if you can provide me with a ride home.

I look forward to your reply.

**Analysis of sample writing for Task 1:**

This essay is an example of a high-scoring response and is a model you want your essay to have followed.  This particular essay has the following factors:

- 169 words
- no grammatical or spelling errors
- appropriate usage of vocabulary
- follows a logical order of information and request

If your essay is similar in nature to the example, you can safely assume a passing score, likely a higher score of 6 or higher.  Be sure to check your spelling and word count, those are the easiest and most common ways to lose points.  (Tip: It is helpful to ask a fellow student, teacher, or friend to read your response as well to see what they think. Sometimes they will have good feedback on whether there is anything you can improve on!)

The question of our society relying more heavily on technology to pay others to complete tasks is an interesting one. For example, in the not too distant past, it would have been unheard of to hire a stranger to go grocery shopping for you but has become normal now.

First, let's explore the positive benefits. The first is that these "app" services on smart phones has created an entire economy. Many people who provide the services are able to generate extra income without having to take another full-time job. It creates flexibility for them to supplement only when they have the time to do so. For the people using the services, they can spend the saved time at their own full-time occupation which could help them generate more income or achieve promotions. It also can help people by allowing them to spend time with their families instead of running errands.

There are however some possible negative consequences. This can be summarized in the fact that society is much faster paced than ever before. This can have negative consequences of people feeling more stress as they become so busy, they are reliant on others to complete what was once a personal chore or responsibility. Becoming dependent on such services creates an expectation it will always be available. For example, if these services discontinue because of new laws, or simply become unaffordable to the user, they could have changed their lifestyle in a way it would be difficult to change back to later.

In summary, the positive benefits of these services outweigh the negative consequences in my opinion, so long as people stay within their means and do not become overly dependent on them.

## Analysis of sample writing for Task 2

The sample response is 282 words long, which is an appropriate length without being too long.

The writing has no spelling or grammatical errors, yet it includes a variety of vocabulary and never repeats the same word needlessly. The context of the vocabulary is appropriate in all situations and contexts, and helps elaborate and emphasize the points of the writer.

The paragraphs are appropriately broken out:

- Paragraph 1, the writer makes a concise and easily understood opening statement. It addresses the question, and even provides a simple example that begins to explore the positive and negative effects asked about.
- Paragraph 2, the writer clearly states they will start with the positive attributes. They provide examples of the benefits for both the "user" and the "provider" of these types of smart phone app services. Very interestingly, they even give an example outside of the scope of money that it could provide personal positive benefits such as spending more time with friends and family. This concisely explores multiple aspects of the question asked.
- Paragraph 3 is approximately the same length as paragraph 2, which is good because it does not rush the comparison and contrast. The writer clearly indicates that the negative effects would most likely be attributed to the "user" of the services, and could have possibly spent another sentence on any possible negative effects on the "provider" of the services.
- Paragraph 4, the writer closes with a concise statement that addresses both points, and concludes succinctly that the positive benefits likely outweigh the negative.

Overall, this essay response would be a very high-scoring essay. This essay would most likely receive a score of 8. A score of 9 is possible, but the lack of addressing negative consequences for the service "providers" could result in a loss of a point.

Printed in Great Britain
by Amazon

78642547R00061